D1092482

BALANCING THE SCALES

BY:

PAPA JOE AVIANCE

Jamie
You ARE ELECTRIC!

All my ♡!

Papa Joe Aviance

Ordering Information:
Quantity sales. Special discounts are available on quantity purchases by corporations, associations, and others.
Orders by U.S. trade bookstores and wholesalers.

Edited and Marketed By
DreamStarters University
www.DreamStartersUniversity.com

Table of Contents

Chapter 1

The Seven Values to Live By

In all of my years on this earth so far, I've learned that there are two basic aspects of life you must attend to and keep in balance in order to live a happy and fulfilling life. The first is your own health and wellness, and the second is your goals and your dreams. Both of these categories are vitally important, and both require motivation and determination.

You might be thinking, "Why focus on just these two aspects of life? Isn't there more to think about and work on?"

The reason this book will focus on these two categories specifically is because when you get them in balance, everything else will fall into place. This has been my experience.

In my life, I've fallen off the path several times. I've lost the balance between taking care of myself and going after what I want, and that's when I found myself faced with some serious challenges, including weighing 450 pounds and being depressed about who I was.

Growing up, my grandparents were my greatest influences. They taught me how to relate to other people and how to succeed as a part of society in my own way. My grandmother taught me how to treat other people, and my grandfather taught me how to work hard and be disciplined.

Together, my grandparents were a dangerous, winning combination. After doing a lot of reflection, I have realized that they taught me seven values that have been instilled in me since I was a child. These seven values are the things that have made me into the man I am today, and that's why I'm going to share them with you here in this very first chapter.

Number one: My grandfather taught me that actions speak louder than words. Enough said!

Number two: I used to always overhear my grandfather telling my mother, "Don't ever be jealous of what others have. If you want it, work for it, and go get it yourself." And true to actions speaking louder than words, this is exactly what I saw my grandfather do throughout his life. If he wanted something, he worked for it until he got it.

Number three: Don't be afraid to speak to anyone— they put their pants on one leg at a time, just like you. Everyone is equally valuable, from the highest paid CEO to the man you pass on the street who is down on his luck.

Number four: Treat others how you want to be treated. Say hello to the janitor the same way you would say hello to someone famous. Treat everyone with respect, even the people who don't deserve it, even your enemies.

Number five: Never use the word "hate" or have hate towards anyone in your heart. You can dislike all you want, but never hate. Hating only hurts you in the end.

Number six: My grandmother would say to me time and time again, "Grandson, listen and listen well. Don't kiss nobody's ass and pay it, too." Meaning, "Don't play the fool."

Number seven: My grandparents taught me to never, ever seek revenge. Let karma handle the dirty work for you. There's no sense in paying somebody back for wronging you. What goes around comes around. You have better things to spend your time on.

If you were to break these seven values down into just one simple instruction, it would sound something like this: Work hard for what you want, be kind to everyone you meet, and don't worry about what other people think of you.

I learned this truth as a child, but as I grew up, as they say, life got in the way. The years passed, and it became easy for me to forget the path my grandparents set me on in the beginning. When I forgot their instruction, it took a toll on me. It negatively affected two major aspects of my life—my health and wellness, and my goals and dreams. To return balance and happiness to my life, I had to return to my roots and remember what was truly important and valuable to me.

This book is designed to help you on your journey through life. In it you will find my story coupled with the lessons I've learned that have brought me to where I am today. I've been fortunate to have so many incredible experiences in my life, including the opportunity to tell my story of dramatic weight loss and life change to a nationwide audience with appearances on *The Doctors* talk show and *The Rachael Ray Show*.

My whole purpose with this book is to give you the tools you need to bring your life into balance. Without balance, you may succeed in one aspect of life but find yourself unable to truly enjoy it. But when you take the balanced approach to life I'm going to outline in this book for you, you will find that you can experience happiness at all stages of your journey, even while working hard to achieve your goals and dreams!

Message

As a kid, my grandparents were a huge influence on my life. They taught me seven values that basically boiled down to: Work hard for what you want, be kind to everyone you meet, and don't worry about what other people think of you. However, I forgot what they taught me as I got older and life got in the way. As result, my life became out of balance, my weight soared up to 450 pounds, and I dealt with serious depression. This book is going to show you how I climbed back to a state of balance, happiness and fulfillment, and how you can, too. It all boils down to taking care of your health and wellness and going after your goals and dreams. I know that no matter where you're at in your journey right now, you can bounce back and have the life you've always wanted. I am living proof.

"Create the highest, grandest vision possible for your life, because you become what you believe!"

Oprah Winfrey

Chapter 2

Start From the Roots

My grandparents were great examples for me to follow. My grandfather used to work in a plant for GM, but after many years, he quit the job and started working for a construction company during the day and a dry cleaners at night.

During this time, he learned everything there was to learn about the construction and dry cleaning business. But as time went on, he began to feel unappreciated and unmotivated. So my grandmother said to him, "If you can work for a boss, then you can do it for yourself!"

Taking her advice, he put a plan together and quit both jobs. His construction boss took him to the bank and helped him get his first loan to start his own remodeling business called Davis Remodeling in Saginaw, Michigan in the late 1960s. For a black man to have his own business at that time was practically unheard of.

He made the front page of the *Saginaw News* several times. One instance was special to me. The caption reads,

BALANCING THE SCALES

"Joe Davis: Loaded With Energy, He's a Doer!" My grandfather framed this and had it hanging in his office. It was the first thing you saw when you walked in the door. I remember I used to stare at this newspaper article in its frame every single day growing up. I re-read it over and over.

I'm named after my grandfather, and we shared a special bond. My grandmother was equally influential. She worked hard at a lot of odd jobs, and then she eventually started her own beauty salon out of the basement of her house. She did all the neighbor's hair and got all the gossip. Not only that, as she worked, she essentially counseled people, including, mostly, my grandfather.

I suffered physical abuse during my childhood and my parents divorced. Before and after the divorce, I stayed with my grandparents on the weekends and holidays, and I eventually lived with them for two years while my mother went to medical school. This gave me the chance to be around my grandmother often as she helped people and her family, and I soaked it all in.

The experiences I had with my grandparents made me who I am today. They are the roots in my life that keep me grounded and moving in a positive direction. My upbringing was definitely not perfect, but I was still given the opportunity to learn good core values.

Your roots are the core values that you live with every day of your life. You have to have some kind of core guiding you forward, or else it is very easy to get distracted by negative influences. I was fortunate to learn this at age three. As I lived with my grandparents through my childhood, I got to see them live out their values firsthand.

One of the things I appreciate the most about my life is being able to watch my grandparents live the lifestyle that I now strive to live. It took me awhile to recognize this, but now that I'm older I can see their positive influence on me as clear as day.

My grandfather rebuilt his city house by house with his business, served as a city councilman for three terms, and he was the school board president to support my mom and uncle in their education and to fight for civil rights within the school district. My grandmother took care of their neighborhood in every way that she could. To put it simply, my grandparents were of service to others.

My grandfather wanted to give back and work hard. As a black man, he had to play the social game very well. Although, when my grandfather closed a deal, he would walk around the house with a big head. My grandmother would quickly put him in check by saying, "Cool your engines, Joe Davis... Nobody knows you 13 miles outside the city!" But for a black man who graduated with an 11th grade education, he did what he had to do, and he appreciated everything that he earned in his life.

BALANCING THE SCALES

My grandparents were both chameleons. Not at all in a bad way. They could dress up or down. They both treated every person they met with respect. A cashier at K-Mart received just as much respect as somebody on the school board.

From observing this, I learned what amazing things kindness can do and what a powerful force it is in the world. You can achieve great things in life when you form connections with other people, and creating lasting connections with others only happens when you treat people right.

Hard work is also important. My family is full of hard workers. As a single mom, my mom started working for my grandfather as his secretary. Then, following the advice of a family friend, my mom decided to go to medical school and became a doctor. I saw her work hard for what she wanted. She wanted to be able to help people, just like my grandparents.

It's in my DNA to be a hard worker as well. I believe my purpose here on earth is to pursue my passions and to be of service to others. I will never give up this way of life because I'm a fighter, and I have been since the day I was born.

You see, I was born three months premature. I weighed three pounds, and I was 12 inches long. I later learned that I was literally kicked into this world. The first time my biological father physically abused my mother was when she was pregnant with me. He kicked her in the stomach, which induced labor and I was born. Doctors didn't think I was going to live.

My lungs were not fully developed, and I was underweight. So underweight that they had to force-feed me through an incubator. My weight dropped to 2.5 lbs. The doctors wouldn't let my parents take me home until I weighed at least 5 lbs or more. I was in the hospital for over three months.

While in the hospital, everyone called me a "miracle baby." My mother was 17 years old when she had me, and the nurses thought she wanted to give me up for adoption. After my health stabilized, the nurses who had taken care of me went to my mom and said, "We'll take the baby."

But my grandmother stood up to them and said, "Like hell you will." And that's how I came into this world. At times I feel like a boxer who is fighting for my life. I'm not in the ring, but my opponent is life itself.

As I fight, I want to inspire others to keep fighting for what they believe in and what they want. When you go back and take a look at your roots, I know you will find what means the most to you and how you really want to live your life. Once you know how you are uniquely positioned to help others, the next step is to work as hard as you can to do so while always remembering that kindness towards others goes a long way.

Message

My grandfather worked hard in his business and wanted to give back to his community in every way that he could. My grandmother helped and counseled others while running a beauty salon out of her basement. My mother, as a single mom, put herself through medical school and became a doctor. Studying my roots has shown me that being a hard worker that helps others is in my DNA. When you study your roots, you too can find out what means the most to you and how you want to live your life. No matter what your path in life is, never forget that showing kindness to everyone that you meet is important. We are all here to make the world a better place.

"Work for it, and GO GET IT YOURSELF!"

My Grandfather

Chapter 3

Self-discovery is a Bitch

My grandparents were a great example for me growing up, but as I got older, I started to rebel. The values my grandparents taught me slipped away. They were still inside of me, but as I went about discovering myself, who I wanted to be and where I fit in the world, they were pushed to the back of my brain.

I wanted to do the opposite of what I had been told to do. I've always been a curious person, and in hindsight I guess I was testing the limits. After screwing up enough times, I eventually realized the error of my ways.

My rebellious quest started around age 11 and lasted until I was about 25 years old. It was a long streak. In some sense, I had my life together because I followed my grandfather and mother's lead as far as my career was concerned.

I applied myself towards figuring that part of life out, but I wasn't happy. It was only six years ago at the time of this writing that I really began to focus on my own happiness. For me, this meant focusing on my health and getting my weight under control, as it was a major reason for my unhappiness.

Even though my grandparents gave me a set of values to guide me in my life, learning how to apply them to my life has been an ongoing process. Now that I'm older, what I learned growing up has come back into play because it now means more to me. My life experience has brought me greater understanding. I often find myself saying, "Oh, that's what my grandparents meant!"

Sometimes the truth of their words will hit me like a ton of bricks. I still look at that newspaper article featuring my grandfather, and every time I do, what he taught me hits me hard. At the bottom of the article, there's a picture of me, my grandma and my grandpa all together that is captioned, "Little Joseph following in his grandfather's footsteps."

I haven't always felt that I've lived up to his standards, but I'm improving every single day, and that's what really counts. All throughout my life, even though I was successful financially, I was miserable inside. I wasn't happy with my relationships. My foundation was weak. There wasn't a lot for me to stand on because I was so unhappy with myself.

I had a good corporate job working on Wall Street, but self-love was something I just never took seriously. Once I had the opportunity to experience it and go through the process of self-discovery, that's when things started to come together for me.

Before I began the process of self-discovery, I didn't think I deserved love. I didn't think I was good enough. I always felt unintelligent, partially because everybody in my family had gone to college, and I left college after two years and never graduated.

That always stuck in my mind, because I have always wanted to make my mom proud. When we went to all of my cousins' graduation ceremonies, I felt horrible and started crying because I felt like I had let my mom down because I didn't finish my degree like she wanted me to.

I didn't finish college because I wanted to get out into the world and experience life. I wanted to start my life and do something with it rather than be in the classroom, but when I left, my conscience still ate at me.

In school growing up, I was bullied because I was a big geek. I played violin. I wasn't into sports. I wasn't one of the popular jocks. But in high school, I taught myself how to go from group to group and make friends with everyone as a survival mechanism.

I've always had a friendly face that says to people, "Tell me your life story," and so I've always attracted other people to me. But I was miserable because I thought of this as a curse. It took me a long time to realize that it was a blessing to have people feel comfortable around me.

BALANCING THE SCALES

In high school, I studied everyone in every group. I studied the jocks, the blacks, the popular, the punks, the preps, the stoners/slackers, the foreigners, the rockers, the class clowns, the mean girls, the geeks/nerds, and the cheerleading squad. Then I pursued and befriended at least two people from each group.

This kept me from being bullied because by knowing someone in every group, if I ever had a problem with somebody, I could go to the people I knew in their group and get backup. It worked like a charm, but I was still miserable because I was exhausting myself by trying to fit in with everyone. I never allowed myself to just be myself.

Even though this was a very difficult time in my life, I learned a lot about people. I befriended people outside of my comfort zone. I learned how they talked and the things they cared about.

As successful as I was with making friends in different groups, I never felt like I really fit in anywhere. I was a band geek, but unfortunately they were the ones who got picked on the most. But I had a love of music growing up and I still have a passion for it.

I didn't know how to channel the energy I was using to try to fit in with everybody into something else. I didn't know how to pull back and use that energy to uncover who I really was.

Now that I'm older, I can see that who I am has been here all along. I'm a people person. This is my strength, and it has served me in so many different ways, including in high school when I had to make friends with everyone to survive. It took me several years to realize that I wouldn't trade my life for anything. I wouldn't trade the experiences I've had for the world. Even though some of them were hard at the time, they've made me who I am today.

If you're struggling right now, let this be a word of encouragement to you. It may take you a long time to uncover your strengths. You may be exhausted and feel like you don't really fit in anywhere. But that's not the truth.

The truth is that whatever you're going through right now is developing you into the person you were meant to be. You might find out, like I have, that what you perceive to be your curse is actually your biggest blessing.

That's right. Self-discovery is a bitch, but I have no doubt that one day you will look back on everything and see how every challenge you've overcome has made you stronger and more uniquely you.

Message

I rebelled against my family and did my own thing for a long time. Inside, I never felt good enough. All throughout my school days, I was bullied. But this forced me to learn how to make friends with all different kinds of people. As a result of trying to fit in with everyone, I felt lost and like I didn't know who I was. It exhausted all of my energy, but I learned a lot. It took me several years to truly appreciate myself for all that I am. In your life, you may feel like you don't belong. You may not like who you are and wish you were someone different. But if you keep going and don't give up on the process of self-discovery, I know you will find that every challenge has made you stronger and more of who you were intended to be.

"No matter who you are, no matter what you did, no matter where you come from, you can always change, become a better version of yourself!"

Madonna

Chapter 4

Changing Through Self-love

After high school and college, I got into the real world of business. This is when my self-destructive actions and eating habits started to get really bad. To put it bluntly, I hated myself. I hated the relationships I was in. I didn't like anything about my life.

I still didn't feel like I fit in with any particular crowd. I couldn't find my tribe, and I felt alone a lot even though I was surrounded by so many people.

I became a slave to the nightlife in the Washington, D.C. and New York City club scenes. I sometimes traveled between states just to party. I started testing the waters of how much energy I could exert before depleting myself. I never stopped to think if I was getting enough rest or if I was eating properly. I didn't take care of myself at all. I just bounced from one thing to the next like a ball in a pinball machine. I never slowed down. I would just walk into a room and say, "Okay, let's go!"

BALANCING THE SCALES

In addition to having to always be "on" for different networking events, parties, and trade shows, I started living a double life. I started using drugs, and my drug use continued to get worse. I tried to manage everything, and I somehow did a decent job, but with all the damage control I had to do, there was little room left for self-discovery.

Everything I do I always do 110%. I've always said, "I'll try anything once, maybe even twice to see if I like it." But my lack of self-control and self-love caused me to get caught up in a downward spiral of depression, drugs and alcohol.

I worked a full-time job on Wall Street as a sales executive for a telecommunications company, and I sold drugs just to keep up with my own habit. I didn't need the money, but I needed the drugs, so selling them meant I always had enough on hand for myself.

I spent a lot of time selling drugs at popular New York and Washington, D.C. nightclubs, and then the next morning I would go into work, sometimes high as a kite, and sit at my desk where I managed 15 different people.

My first real job after I left college, I worked for a big company in the computer industry at the height of its success. I got my job there by starting off in the billing department. Within one year, I used my networking skills to become an assistant producer in their computing department.

I had been going to school for communications, radio and TV broadcasting, but I broke into computers because this was in the early 90s when they were the hot new technology. Using my people skills, I networked my way into a great position as the business development manager and I had the chance to travel the world and recruit big name clients.

I was accomplishing a lot in the corporate world, but it didn't change the way I felt about myself. I didn't like anything about myself, and I had an addiction to food and drugs.

My depression lasted for a very long time because I didn't seek medical attention. I just faked like I was okay until I could escape in drugs or in my job. Even though I was excelling tremendously, everything sucked. I was making so much money, but I loathed myself and depression had its grip on me.

I knew deep down that I had to make a decision to change, but I didn't do it for a long time. I laughed at the people I saw on television talk shows who had lost a bunch of weight. At the time, I couldn't bring myself to even try to change, so I just laughed at the people who had while stuffing my face with burritos.

My definition of self-love is being able to look at yourself in the mirror and love yourself. Unfortunately, I used to run from the mirror. I mean that literally because I used to only ever use a mirror to make sure I didn't have food on my shirt. I didn't like what I saw. Every time I went to the store, I had to buy bigger and bigger clothes.

BALANCING THE SCALES

Looking back, I can see that I was giving my energy to the wrong things throughout this time period in my life. I didn't have my priorities straight. Yeah, I was making a lot of money, but I couldn't fully enjoy it because I didn't have my health. I was also wasting a lot of my time taking drugs and selling them, which left very little time for me to really think about how I was hurting myself or how I could change.

I didn't learn the importance of putting my energy to use in the right channels until just 11 years ago when I moved from New York to LA to pursue being an actor. My first agent was the one who told me, "Don't give all your energy away in the audition room. If you do, then you'll have nothing left for the casting director when they see you."

Something just clicked when she told me this, and I realized there was a deeper message to what she was saying for my life overall. I spent so much time caught up in going from one thing to the next that I never slowed down and thought about what I was spending my energy on. In reality, I was spending my energy on trying to forget how miserable I was, and that was a bad cycle to be caught up in.

Turning my life around was a process of applying my energy and focus to the right areas of my life that I neglected for so long. When you're giving your life to all the wrong things, and you feel horrible because of it, you have to realize you're not broken. You're not fundamentally flawed and unlovable.

What has happened is you've put your energy into the wrong channels that are no longer serving you, and this has caused your life to get out of balance. The way to turn things around is to focus on self-love, and from there you can begin to make different choices, prioritize what really matters to you right now, in this moment, and begin your process of incredible transformation.

Message

When I left college, I put everything I had into my career, but I stopped taking care of myself. I developed a drug addiction and a food addiction, and I never slowed down. I was "on" 24/7, and I went from one thing to the next. I was making a ton of money, but I could hardly enjoy it because I hated myself. The only way I could turn things around was through self-love. If you're struggling, I believe it's because you've put your energy into the wrong channels like I did, and your life has become out of balance. But you can restore the balance by prioritizing what really matters to you, making different, better choices, and loving yourself through the process of transformation.

"Fall down seven times, stand up eight!"

Japanese Proverb

Chapter 5

Remember What Makes You Happy

In 2009, I was working in a video store, and a DJ came up to me and said, "I like your voice. I would love to record it. You have a great voice for dance music." His name was Eddie Amador, and he was about to change my life.

I was very into dance music when I participated in the New York City and Washington, D.C. nightclub scenes, so for Eddie to say something like this to me immediately got my attention. Eddie also told me that he was throwing a party, and he wanted me to host it. I agreed. It went well, and the next thing I knew, Eddie had recorded a track he wanted me to write lyrics for and record vocals on.

The song went on to be signed by KULT Records (Live it, Love it, NOW!) very quickly. Then the label contacted me and said, "Before we put out this track, we're going to partner you with another artist on our label for another song." The artist was Lula, who I knew from when I used to dance to her tracks in the nightclubs.

BALANCING THE SCALES

The song we did together is called "Last Night a DJ Saved My Life," and we also did a video for it. A week later, the label contacted me and told me the song was going to become a top *Billboard* dance hit. The song was up against all of the heavy hitters like Christina Aguilera, Britney Spears, and Beyoncé, and it eventually made it to number six on the charts.

It started off right away on the charts at number 24. When I saw that, that was the moment I decided I absolutely needed to change my life. When I saw myself in the music video, I was embarrassed. There's a clip in the video a little over four minutes into it that to this day I can't stand to watch. It's just a reminder for me of how I let my weight get out of control.

Growing up, people called me all sorts of different names like Big Joe and Big Papa. They always included that word—"big." It was never just Joe.

The day the label told me, "We want you to be like the next Biggie Smalls for house music," I knew it was either I make a transformation, or I was going to become something in the public eye that I didn't want to become. I didn't want to be known for my size. I wanted to be known for my vocal talents.

So I told the label, "No, I don't want to be that. That's not who I am." This phone call was my wake up call. I decided it was time for me to break up with food. By this time, I had already broken away from drugs on my own. I knew I had the strength to change. It was just a matter of making it a priority and focusing on it.

Music was a passion of mine growing up. I felt very fortunate for it to be circling back around into my life. But I didn't like that the label was trying to pigeonhole me into being someone that I didn't see myself as.

Even though this good thing was happening to me, I was still miserable, and I knew I couldn't allow myself to just stay that way. I felt a lot of pressure to change. I didn't have diabetes, high cholesterol or any other diseases, but I felt like I was two cheeseburgers away from having a heart attack. My mental health was no better.

I had stopped doing what I was passionate about for a long time, and the joy was drained out of my life. There was a big gap of time between when I did music in high school and when my song became a *Billboard* hit. In the absence of music, drugs and food had taken over as my passions. I was listening to music, but I wasn't making any. The opportunity to make music again inspired me to finally remove food from center stage in my life.

Once I aligned with my passion for music again, I lost 250 pounds by walking and eating healthy. I didn't go to the gym twice a day. I didn't have gastric bypass surgery. I didn't do any crazy diets. I just changed my eating habits by shopping at 99 Cents Only Stores.

37

BALANCING THE SCALES

Once I was reminded of what really made me happy in life, I had enough motivation to change. My passion for life was ignited again at just the right moment.

When I say the word "passion," what I mean is something that makes you feel good in your heart. That could be anything. We all have different passions. For some it's playing sports, building things, doing research, or helping others in a medical profession.

Whatever makes your heart sing is your passion, but it's up to you to pursue it in your life. There may be many times in your life that you will become distracted and not make time for what you love. When this happens, it is easy fall into destructive habits and patterns.

When we don't make our passion our purpose, our lives easily get out of balance because we are left with a void to fill. This void can only be filled by getting back on your true path and by practicing self-love.

I didn't begin to experience self-love until I found my passion for music again after having lost it for years. When music came back into my life, I made the decision to change because I saw the opportunity for me to do something that I loved, and I wanted to rise to the occasion.

If you're feeling unmotivated, flat or downright unhappy, maybe it is time for you to reconnect with what you love so your drive to live life can be restored. When you remember what makes you happy, I know you will be given the strength to change for the better!

Message

For many years, I lost touch with my passion for life. This left me with a void in my heart, and I filled it with food and drugs. When I had the opportunity to do music again, something that I once loved, I knew it was time for me to make a change to improve my health and get reconnected with myself. If you're unhappy with where you're at in your life, take time to remember what you love—your passion. When you're doing what you're passionate about, it will give you the strength to get away from negative habits and change your life in a positive way.

"Always go with your passions. Never ask yourself if it's realistic or not!"

Deepak Chopra

Chapter 6

Shake What Your Mama Gave You

Who are you? What are your talents? What are you passionate about? What do you believe in? What are your strengths? What makes you, you?

There are many different types of people in this world. That's one of the things I enjoy most about studying people. We are the most fascinating creatures on this planet. I've always enjoyed learning about others.

One of my strengths is my listening skills. I've worked directly with people for so long throughout my life that I'm at the point where I can have three conversations at once, and I can still hear a pin drop across the room.

The way I view listening to and interacting with people is that every human being is like a radio station. We're all broadcasting different things, and we're all tuned in to different channels on different wavelengths. Some people have difficulty getting on the same wavelength with other people, but this is something I've mastered.

BALANCING THE SCALES

One of my strengths is being able to tune in to different channels, listen and build rapport with people. As you know, I didn't always value this ability in myself, but over time I've learned it's one of the things that makes me unique.

I watched my grandparents live like chameleons, and I saw what establishing good relationships with other people could accomplish. I took this with me into high school.

With the jocks, I played the jock. With the band geeks, I played the band geek. By doing this, I learned to appreciate that every person I met was unique. They all had different gifts and talents. I got to witness that up close and personal by getting to know so many different people.

I thought it was a curse to be an approachable, relatable person back then, but now I see it as a blessing, and I appreciate it even more. Not everyone can easily relate to all different kinds of people, but it's something I'm good at. It's my gift.

If you have a gift, embrace it. Shake what your mama gave you. Otherwise, you're wasting the talents God has given you. I don't believe anyone can become really successful or happy if they hide the best, most unique parts about themselves from the world. These are the things that make you, you, and your mission on this earth can't be completed by anyone else.

Most people spend a lot of their lives wondering who they are. But, paradoxically, they try to find themselves by letting the world define them and who they should be. This never works because who you are can't be discovered by looking outside. Who you are can only be found by looking inside. Looking inside is part of the journey of self-discovery.

I've learned that a lot of people are fearful of really examining themselves, who they are and who they have been. They're afraid of accepting responsibility, and they are scared to hold themselves accountable for their actions.

They don't want to believe that their choices have taken them in one direction or another, and instead they give up responsibility for their own lives. Sadly, it's not just responsibility they are giving up when this happens. They're also giving up their own power.

What happens when someone lives life like this is they put on a fake persona. They try to hide who they are from other people, and in the process they forget who they are themselves. This is what playing the fool looks like, and I'm thankful my grandmother taught me to avoid this in my life, no matter how long it took me to fully understand what she meant.

I believe we create ourselves by the choices we make, and these choices either lead us closer or further away from who we truly are. Whether they know it or not, many people are trying to find themselves, but they are miserable because they're looking in all the wrong places. They're looking in the wrong places because something is off balance, and it needs to be addressed.

To avoid being caught in this trap, you've got to put yourself in front of the mirror and ask yourself honestly what is going on. You've got to get to the root of the problem, and you can't be afraid of what you're going to find when you go digging. What you will uncover by looking at yourself this way is the good within you that you need to embrace, and the bad within you that you need to get rid of.

I'm not saying this process is easy or that it can be done overnight. It's difficult to do, and it requires courage to accept that our problems are often of our own creation. But it's the best way to come to full acceptance of yourself and all that you're truly capable of. Ask yourself, "Who do I want to be?"

I've got to be honest, I'm in my 40s, and I still don't have the perfect answer to this question for every aspect of my life. But you don't have to have the perfect answer for this question for it to guide you and the choices you make in your life. The question of who you want to be is an ongoing one, and the beautiful thing about life is that you always have the opportunity to learn and grow and keep defining who you want to be.

Life isn't about "getting there" as much as it is about enjoying where you are right now. Don't become too excited about what is to come and lose your passion for what's happening now. Don't miss out on enjoying the little steps along the way.

Most of all, embrace who you are. Just be you, right now, from here on forward!

Message

One of my biggest strengths is my ability to listen to people, learn about them and build a relationship with them. Through this, I've learned that everyone is unique, and we all have different gifts and talents. Many people do themselves a disservice when they try to hide who they are from everyone else or when they let the world define them. If you are searching for yourself, you have to look at yourself in the mirror honestly and have the courage to accept responsibility for your life. Ask yourself, "Who do I want to be?" This question will guide you throughout your life. Embrace who you are, and enjoy every step of the journey of becoming more and more who you were uniquely designed to be!

"Be yourself; everyone else is taken!"

Oscar Wilde

Chapter 7

What is Your Why?

One of the things I had to do as a food addict was figure out why I was eating so much junk food. To help myself slow down and stop acting merely out of habit, I learned to ask myself what I call "the three Ws." The three Ws are what, when and why.

Whenever I found myself reaching for junk food, I'd slow down and ask myself: What are you eating? When are you eating it? Why are you eating it? I found that the most important of these questions for me was the why.

By really looking at why I was eating something, I realized that a lot of my eating was driven by my emotions. I didn't eat because I was hungry. If I was in a bad emotional state for some reason, then I would deal with it by eating junk.

I noticed a negative pattern that my eating habits followed. When something made me upset, I ate. When somebody pissed me off, I ate. Once I targeted this, I realized that I was in control and that I didn't have to let my emotions dictate my actions.

BALANCING THE SCALES

Instead of grabbing for the chocolate cake when somebody cut me off in traffic, I learned to observe my feelings and let myself calm down naturally. Then it became easy for me resist the temptation to eat when provoked. I could just say to myself, "Okay, I don't need to eat this. I'm good."

My eating habits were so bad prior to this that the people working at McDonald's knew my voice when I went through the drive through. I'd go through and they'd say, "Hey, Papa Joe, the usual?" "The usual" was two Big Macs, two large fries and two diet Cokes.

A late night binge session consisted of this meal from McDonald's, plus a whole chocolate cake, a family sized bag of Doritos, and a two-liter bottle of Mountain Dew. I drank a two-liter bottle of Mountain Dew every single day for five years when I was working in New York.

Eating like this is what caused my weight to climb higher and higher. But it took me a long time before I was willing to acknowledge that I had a problem.

I've always been an adventurous thrill seeker. One of my favorite things to do is ride roller coasters. I absolutely love them, so one summer when my weight was at its peak, I joined a roller coaster club and traveled to different amusement parks within the U.S. I had the awesome opportunity of getting to go experience all of these roller coasters, and then I would give my review of them to the Travel Channel.

On one of my trips, I went to Six Flags and tried to get on a roller coaster there in the front seat. I had an extender put on to buckle me in, but it wouldn't fit. What happened next destroyed me.

The ride attendant said to me, "Sir, I'm so sorry. You're too fat to ride this ride." Everyone around us went quiet. You could hear a pin drop, and then everyone started laughing.

I started crying. I got off the ride. I walked down to the concession stand, and I grabbed a foot long hot dog, some fries and a Coke. It was the only thing I knew to do to deal with the embarrassment of being laughed at for being too big for the roller coaster. Food was my coping mechanism, but instead of giving me any relief from my problems, it just created more.

Even after this experience, I still didn't want to change my eating habits. I was still fearful of changing myself. I had no motivation. I was stuck in my old habits, and I was depressed.

I hadn't really taken care of myself for many, many years. On top of that, I was extremely emotionally sensitive. I let the stresses of the world get to me on a daily basis, and that was difficult because I'm really a people person. I care about other people a lot.

But when you combine that with not caring for yourself, it's extremely exhausting. I used to listen to every single sob story that somebody would tell me. Emotionally, I would take on other people's problems and try to fix them myself. I didn't even realize how much this was affecting me personally.

I would come away from interactions with people feeling angry, confused, mad and sad, and it took a lot out of me. What was being taken out of me I tried to put back by comforting myself with food.

Now that I understand the importance of my emotions when it comes to food, I have a whole new approach to taking care of my health. Losing 275 pounds didn't happen just because I decided I wanted to start eating differently. That's only one part of the story. Being able to lose the weight and keep it off happened because I decided to give my whole life a makeover from the emotional level to the physical level.

Before I made the decision to get healthy, the world was playing me, and I wasn't playing it. I used to eat 7,000 calories a day. But now junk food doesn't even come into play. Because I have transformed my life on the deepest level, I've mastered how to not even think about falling into my old eating habits.

That doesn't mean that making the change was easy. In fact, I had a nervous breakdown the day I decided to change my life and break up with food. I went to the fridge and threw out everything that was going to get in my way of losing weight. It was very difficult to do because for so long food played a huge part in my life. I was literally left with a bottle of ketchup, a bottle of mustard, and some relish.

But having discovered the why that was at the back of all of my eating habits, I was able to push through and change my life for good. If you have a negative habit that is dragging your life down the wrong path, first find out why you keep returning to it. What are your triggers? What purpose is the negative habit serving in your life?

When you understand this, then you are on the path to lasting change. You will no longer be forced to use just your willpower to change your habit. When you understand the cause or "why" of the issue, you can change the source of the issue. It's hard work, but I can assure you it's worth it!

"If you're strong enough to lift up a weight, then you're strong enough to control what's on your plate."

Unknown

Chapter 8

Keep It Simple Stupid

After I decided I was going to make a change in my eating habits, because I had no nutritional background, I decided to keep things very simple. At the time in my life when I decided to make a change, I was unemployed, and I couldn't afford to go to a gym. I couldn't afford to join a weight loss program or a food service. So what I did was I took a look at the food pyramid, familiarized myself with the recommended guidelines for what I should be eating, and decided I would follow them as closely as possible.

A friend recommended I shop at 99 Cents Only Stores. At first, I turned up my nose like a snob at the idea of shopping at a discount store for my groceries. I figured they wouldn't have much of a selection to choose from. But with no money coming in, my budget was minimal. I decided it wouldn't hurt to go in and look around.

I was pleasantly surprised to find that at these stores I could buy all the basics of a healthy diet including fresh fruits and vegetables. When I first walked into the store and started to look around, something just clicked for me. It was like a white light came shining down from heaven and I just knew that I was on the right track.

I knew that if I committed myself to eating right, I was going to get healthy, even on my limited budget. So I began shopping at the 99 Cents Only Stores to buy food for all of my meals. In total, I spent about $40 a week for food, and it was all high quality and nutritious.

To give you an idea of what I ate, my breakfast usually consisted of a spinach omelet, some wheat toast, and some fruit on the side with two big bottles of water. For lunch I ate a salad with tuna in it or any type of garden salad. For dinner I generally ate some kind of protein like chicken, fish or beef and a vegetable. Keeping things simple was how I made sure I could keep eating healthy long-term.

When I ate out at restaurants, I gave up french fries and mashed potatoes. Instead, I went for two orders of vegetables. When I wanted a snack, I went for something that would make me feel full like nuts.

I still had a sweet tooth, but instead of eating a whole chocolate cake, I limited it to just one slice. Instead of bingeing on candy and sweets, when I wanted something like that, I would buy snack size peanut M&Ms, and I learned to enjoy just eating what was in that small bag and then being done.

It was torture at first for me to limit myself when it came to these kinds of foods. But over time my self-discipline improved. I still bought whole chocolate cakes to put in my fridge, but I told myself, "You're only going to eat one slice at a time, and that's it." I knew I had to learn to control my bad eating habits consistently for my weight loss to last. I knew I had to change my relationship with food.

I started telling myself, "Food was a bad best friend." I didn't allow it any longer to be something I relied on for comfort or even entertainment. I created a simple, healthy eating plan based off of the food pyramid, and I stuck to it. I didn't buy into any fad diets or try to take any shortcuts. My weight didn't get up to 450 pounds overnight, and I knew it wouldn't come off that fast, either.

I didn't try to track every single bite of food that I ate, but I made a commitment to making smarter choices. To be honest, before I really made the decision to change, I had tried every single type of special diet out there, but none of them stuck for me. Drinking special shakes for half of my meals didn't appeal to me, and I didn't have the money for that either.

In my opinion, fad diets almost never work long-term. A lot of times we even find out later that they're completely unhealthy. I'd already bounced around from diet to diet for many years, but I always got disappointing results and quit because they were too restrictive and not realistic for anyone to do forever.

By putting my own plan together, I was able to eat food that I actually liked and wouldn't get bored with. I decided to stick to the way I was eating for six months and see where it got me. I also committed to forming new habits so I could create and maintain a new lifestyle.

I prepared my meals in bulk. For example, I would cook up a big pot of rice and beans or a big stew and break that up into five different servings to keep in the fridge. This way, I knew exactly what I was going to eat every day, and I didn't have to spend much time thinking about it. By doing this, I also learned how to be happy and satisfied with what I had.

After six months, if I wanted to cheat, then I told myself I could, but I made rules for myself. If I wanted to go get a Big Mac at McDonald's, then the rule was I had to walk there, and I couldn't eat until I got back home. In this way, if I wanted to indulge, I had to do the work of walking first.

By making myself wait until I got back home to eat, this also helped me limit how much I would eat. The burger would get cold and not taste as good, so it was easier for me to not eat the whole thing.

I lost my first 20 pounds as soon as I quit drinking soda. And within the first six weeks, I lost 35 pounds. I woke up every single morning at 7 o'clock like clockwork for 18 months to do my morning walks. In this timeframe, I lost 250 pounds, and I've lost 25 since then for a total of 275. At 250 pounds down, that's when recognition started coming in from network TV.

But I wasn't trying to lose weight for recognition. It was all for me. For a long time, I wanted to stay out of the spotlight as much as possible. I was too embarrassed to even go to a gym. I started walking for exercise because I said to myself, "What's the easiest exercise I can do?"

Walking was the answer, so I grabbed my tennis and my dance music, and I hit the streets. I knew that on the streets if people were looking at me or criticizing me, I wouldn't hear them. I was in my own bubble. I couldn't be judged because if you pass me in your car, you're going to whiz past me in two seconds. I had a fear of people staring at me, but this is how I overcame it.

I only increased the distance I was walking when my song went up on the *Billboard* chart. When it went up, I would walk to a farther newsstand to get the *Billboard* magazine and bring it back as a keepsake. It was my reward for walking.

When I decided to start walking, it was following a period where I was so depressed for two months that I didn't leave my apartment and had food delivered. I had just gone through a bad breakup of seven years, and I had just lost my job. I was on my own.

But the people I passed on the sidewalks each morning started to become like my support group. They were the ones

I showed love to because they were the ones out trying to better themselves just like me. When I took a day off, which was rare, the people I normally saw on my route would check on me. They'd say, "Hey, I didn't see you the other day. Where've you been?"

Through my own determination and this kind of positive support, I started to find the superhero within me, which I call the Electric Negro. I started calling myself this, and soon my whole neighborhood knew me by that name. I even created a shirt that's now part of my clothing line that says "Electric Negro" on it, and I wore that out on my walks.

I became so comfortable in my own skin that I could stand on the corner and groove to my music without fear of anyone judging me. I didn't care what other people thought of me, because I was just being myself. Keeping things simple, creating my own plan and sticking to it is what has brought me to where I am today.

No matter what you're trying to achieve, whether it's weight loss, weight gain, or something else entirely, the best plan of action is your own. Of course, it's great to have some guidance, but you know yourself best. You know what will work for you. Don't overcomplicate things. Keep them simple, and you will be amazed by what you can achieve.

Message

When I decided it was time for me to make a change in regards to my weight, I kept things simple. I created my own weight loss plan based on basic nutritional guidelines, and I did the easiest exercise I could think of—walking. In 18 months, by sticking to my plan consistently, I effectively lost 250 pounds. If there's something that you want to achieve in your life, whether that's weight loss, weight gain, or some other kind of transformation, the best plan is the simple one which you will stick with long-term. You have to do what's right for you, and you know yourself best. It's great to follow the guidance of others, but unless you are willing to commit to a plan of action, transformation is impossible. You will be amazed by what you can achieve by following a very simple plan in your life!

"You'll thank yourself 3 months from now!"

Unknown

Chapter 9

Two Suitcases and a Dream

In 2001, I was living in New York, but jobs were hard to come by in the city after 9/11. So I decided that I needed to make a life change and move somewhere new. I had been out to California a couple of times for business and loved it, and I had a friend in LA who offered to let me live with him.

So I boarded a red-eye flight and made my way to LA. My friend picked me up from the airport the night I got in, and I already had a job interview lined up for the very next day. I was ready to hustle and hit the ground running.

I got going early the next morning. I'd never used the transit system in LA before, and I had to make a series of transfers in order to get to my job interview on time. It was seriously stressful, but I figured it out and made it to my interview.

I walked out the door with the job in hand. When I left the interview, I went back to my friend's place, and I found my suitcases out on the porch. I had no clue what was going on. I knocked on the door, which was locked, and soon my "friend" answered it.

He told me, "I decided I don't want to have a roommate," and then he shut the door in my face. This is how I became homeless in LA on my second day in the city. There was nobody I could call on for help, and I didn't know my way around the city very well, so I went to the Saharan Motor Hotel on Sunset Boulevard and checked myself in.

That night at 3 a.m. there was a knock on my door. I didn't answer because it was so late, and after a couple more knocks, the door to my room was broken down. The LAPD stormed in, put a 9-millimeter handgun in my mouth, and said, "Are you Lonnie?"

I was so startled all I could get out was, "No." The officer asked me more questions, and I answered them all with the gun in my mouth.

All of the sudden, I heard from outside, "Wrong room. He's over here."

Then the officer pulled the gun away, walked to the door, and left saying, "Sorry, have a good night."

This was my welcome to LA. The next morning, I went to the front desk and spoke to the manager of the hotel. I knew I was going to have to stay in the hotel for a while, so I needed to see what kind of deal I could get for an extended stay. When I told the manager about what had happened the night before, he offered me two weeks for free, and he gave me a mini fridge and hot plate to use.

This was a huge blessing. I was in survival mode. I didn't even know how I was going to get through the next couple of days prior to this. Mentally, I was a wreck, and I was wondering if I'd even made the right choice to move to LA.

I ended up living in the hotel for four months, and I acclimated to hotel living pretty quickly because I had done so much traveling throughout my career prior to going to LA. I was very fortunate to get outside of my bubble, experience different cultures and see different parts of the world while traveling for business. I've always considered the earth my classroom, and I believe the world doesn't see you until you see it.

Whenever I travel, I love to get lost on purpose and try to find my way back. This is a great way to really immerse yourself in a new culture and new surroundings. Whenever I traveled for business, I always learned how to say hello and goodbye in whatever language was spoken where I was visiting. This shows you're making an effort to get to know the people and the culture where you are.

When I was depressed and struggling with my weight, it was a happy release for me to be able to go and see the world. It didn't change the fact that I was depressed and overweight, but it kept me going. It gave me a sense of relief from the day-to-day things that I struggled with.

69

BALANCING THE SCALES

A change of scenery can make a big impact on your outlook. It's easy to get stuck in patterns and routines if you only know the environment you've been in for years. There's so much more out there in the world to see, experience and explore. When you see and experience new things with your own eyes, sometimes this is enough to unlock the limited mindset you may have adopted for yourself.

You may not want to move to LA or travel across the world, but experiencing new things in your life will help you get out of your bubble, open your mind and start dreaming of the possibilities for your life. If there's somewhere you'd love to visit, put a plan together and go make it happen!

There's more to the world than the four walls you live within every day. I left my comfort zone for LA with two suitcases and a dream, and it's paid off in so many ways, even though it started off in the worst way possible. The journey to where I am now has been hard, but it's also been exciting, mind-opening and totally worth it. I have no doubt that whatever you do and wherever you go will be just as exciting and adventuresome!

Message

I left New York for LA with two suitcases and a dream, and when I arrived I found myself homeless, wanted for a some crime I didn't commit, and totally unsure if I'd made the right decision to leave my former life behind. But before long, I acclimated to my new life situation, and I'm grateful for all the opportunities that living in LA has provided me with. I've found that travel of all kinds is a great way to expand your mind and change your outlook on the world. If there's somewhere you've always wanted to visit or even live, put a plan together and act on it. The world won't see you until you see it. So get out there and have an adventure!

"The biggest adventure you can take is to live the life of your dreams!"

Oprah Winfrey

Chapter 10

Sell Yourself to Be Yourself

This chapter is for anybody who is looking to further their career or start something new as an entrepreneur or business leader. Whether you're looking for investors or partners to finance a project, or looking for someone to hire you to do the work of your dreams, there's one thing to remember: It's not so much your product or your skills that people are investing in, it's you.

This is why becoming skilled at networking is so important. Networking to me is about first impressions. Whenever I've been on the job hunt in my life, I've been lucky to be able to pick out a job I'd like to have, hand in my resume, get an interview and generally walk out of the interview with an offer in hand. This ability stems from my personality and experience, knowing how to ask the right questions, and knowing what I want to get out of a job.

In life, you have to know how to sell yourself. We live in a social world, so a big part of being able to sell yourself is not so much about you as it is about the people you surround yourself with. Who you know and who knows you plays a big role in the opportunities you will have open to you in your life in terms of your career. This is just the way it is.

Unfortunately, in my life, I've surrounded myself with both the good and the bad. I've seen both sides of what happens when you have the right connections in the right places, and what happens when you have the wrong connections in the wrong places. As a drug dealer in the 90s, I got myself into some sticky situations. But I also learned skills I've applied to the corporate world—"street smarts," if you want to call them that.

When it comes to job hunting or hunting for partners and investors for your own business, you have to know how to figure out what the employer, investor or potential partner is looking for, and decide if you are the one who can give it to them. If you can, then you've got to articulate that in a way that they can understand.

If you're replying to a job post, this is about as simple as it gets. In the job description, you're told exactly what the company is looking for, and your job is to tailor your resume to fit their description. If you can read between the lines and understand the hole the company is trying to fill, you can position yourself to fill it.

This is also a very important concept when it comes to networking and sales. My background is in sales, and the key to sales is understanding your customer's pain. If you can offer them a solution to their pain, then you are well positioned to make a sale. A bond is created when you can understand where someone is at, and offer them something that helps them get to where they want to go.

This also applies to everyday relationships, including the relationships you have with friends and family. When you help people solve their problems in any context, it creates a lasting bond. Some people in my Rolodex I have worked with for over 20 years. We've helped each other in various ways over the years, and I can still call on them when needed.

One thing you've got to understand is that doing good business is not about having one-off success. I understand that if you're an entrepreneur, then you're a go-getter, and you have it in your spirit to want things to be done fast. But business is never about getting what you want and then pushing people aside. It's about valuing people.

The best way to build your network is through valuing people, even the people you don't think could do anything for you. You never know how someone may be able to help you or you help them in the future.

In every job that I've ever had, I've offered my help to people when they needed it. Relationships are the cornerstone of business. Even when I sold drugs, I had friends I knew I could count on even though they were addicts.

Building your network is about building trust with other people. I take pride in being a trustworthy individual because I know the value of trust in relationships is huge, and I believe that every connection with another individual is a good connection.

Building your network is about both giving and accepting help. This creates balance in your relationships. People will come and go throughout your life. It's a big world out there, and not everybody is going to hang on and stay in your circle. But you have to be open to having a long-term relationship.

At one point in my career, I had the opportunity to meet with the vice president of a huge insurance company. We went out to lunch together to talk business, and we bonded instantly.

Years down the road, when I moved to LA and was stuck in the hotel I mentioned in the last chapter, I wasn't sure how I was going to cover the bill. So I called this man up and said, "I'm so sorry to ask you this, but can I borrow $300?" I explained to him the situation I was in, and he wired me the money.

I was so thankful. I didn't hear from this man again for a long time until one day I received a message from him on Facebook. He had seen me on *The Rachael Ray Show* talking about my weight loss, and he wanted some advice from me on how he could lose weight, too. It was my pleasure to help him and return the favor he had done for me in my own way. This is the value of building relationships with people, and it all comes from being willing to ask for and give help to other people.

Everyone hates the word sales. It has such a negative connotation to it. But seen in another light, sales is just about being the person who's willing to connect other people to what they need. Sometimes it's you who needs to sell yourself to get a job to support yourself, or to get help from a friend when you're in need. This is what I mean when I say you've got to sell yourself to be yourself.

When you connect with others in a meaningful way, good things happen. Your network is one of your most valuable assets. Take time to build it the right way by giving help and receiving help in return, and you will reap the rewards over time.

Message

Networking plays an important role in business, no matter if you're searching for a job or looking for investors or partners for a new project. Building your network means building long-term relationships with people. Some of my contacts I've worked with for over 20 years, and I know I can still count on them. You can build a network like this for yourself by offering to help others, and by being willing to receive help from others when you need it. People often think of "sales" as a negative thing, but it's really just connecting a person with a product or service that is going to help them solve a problem. When you learn to understand people's pain and know how to help them get rid of it, you become valuable to them. This is the basis for most meaningful relationships. If you take time to build your network the right way, it will require you to do some "selling" of yourself, but the rewards will be worth it.

"You don't close a sale; you open a relationship!"

Patricia Fripp

Chapter 11

Cutting Teeth

In my life, I make it a point to appreciate everything I have. I know what the ultimate goal looks like for me, but I take time to appreciate the smaller victories.

To me, life is really about taking a step back and appreciating what's already happened for you. That's what keeps me positive. I'm thankful to have social media because I can go back and look at my pictures and think, "Man, you've done a lot." I have had so many experiences since moving to LA, and I know that everything I've done has just been a part of my progression.

The first step to beginning to move in a new direction is deciding where you want to go. What excites you? What's in your heart? What have you visualized experiencing? What type of experience are you looking for? You may have to face some fears to get to where you want to be, but even this you can be thankful for because it means you're growing.

The very first public speech I ever gave was for the American Heart Association in front of 5,000 people. I had been on TV before, but having 10,000 eyeballs staring back at me was something I hadn't experienced. It was totally nerve-wracking, but it helped me grow. I went on to become the lifestyle change ambassador for the American Heart Association. A few years later, I also became the brand ambassador for the 99 Cents Only Stores.

I wouldn't have had the confidence to take on these roles if I hadn't been putting myself out there as a speaker. When I gave my first speech for the American Heart Association, I was terrified. Honestly, it didn't come out the way I wanted it to, and I criticized myself because I was expecting to be an excellent speaker right off the bat.

But if I hadn't had this experience, I wouldn't have learned what it takes to be a great speaker. This is why I appreciate every opportunity I have to do something new. I have gratitude for every time I've only done something half as good as I wanted to, because I know that means I'm one step closer to being great at it.

In life, you might be given more than you can handle, but everything you do will prepare you for the next step. When you give everything 100% effort, you put yourself in the best possible position to succeed not just right now but also in the future.

I wasn't prepared to speak to a crowd of 5,000 people, but I put together a speech as best as I could, and I showed up to deliver it. As bad as I thought I did, I ended up getting hired to emcee every American Heart Association walk for the rest of that year. The result was I got to share my story and inspire thousands of people.

I may have expected to be like Tony Robbins immediately, but I had to cut my teeth on public speaking first. Through speaking regularly, I came to appreciate the process of learning as you go to gain new skills.

This is one reason why I've always loved working for small, startup companies. Having worked for bigger companies before, I learned that I didn't want to just be a number that is responsible for a very specific, predictable task. Smaller companies give you the opportunity to learn and gain insights on so many levels because you get to develop and create your own role and responsibilities as you go.

For me, this is one of the most exciting things about life. We all have the ability to define our roles and who we want to be as we go.

I didn't know I was going to do bigger things when I was going through depression and feeling stuck in my corporate career. But when I realized I needed to pursue something different, that's when the wheels started to spin in a different direction.

I had to keep pushing forward. I wanted to pursue acting, and even though I kept getting auditions for roles I wasn't interested in, one day I wound up going in for an audition for a Disney commercial.

As I was leaving the audition, I heard the casting director say, "He's not right for this one." I was disappointed, to say the least. But as I was walking down the hall to leave, I walked past three other doors, not knowing that Disney was doing auditions for four different commercials that day.

As I walked past the final door, I heard somebody say, "Hey, you. Come here." When I walked into the room, there in front of me was a casting director and a producer, and they wanted me to try out for a role.

I agreed to try it, and when I left they told me, "We really like your look. We'll be in touch." The thing that's crazy about this is the role was originally intended for a white guy, and about 500 different people had tried out for it. I was the only black guy who auditioned, and I got the role.

The point I'm trying to make is you just never know what's around the corner for you. I left my first audition that day feeling like I had hit a wall, but by the grace of God, a sign that I should continue on the path I was on showed up.

Disney liked the commercial we made so much it became the station ID for their channel. Before their main programming came on, this commercial would run. It ran for three years, and it was even used for their New Year's Eve programming.

It was a little win for me, but it kept me moving in the right direction. It taught me an important lesson that everything can turn around in a second.

BALANCING THE SCALES

This is why you should never give up. Opportunity will come to you if keep searching for it. You will face rejection, but when you do, just remember that it's nothing against you. It just means whatever you were trying to do wasn't meant for you. They're just saying no to a name, not to you personally.

So no matter what you're trying to accomplish, allow yourself to get really deep down and dirty. Learn the ins and outs. Listen with humility and realize that every step you take is a step that will ultimately take you in the right direction if you never give up.

Message

The first time I spoke to a crowd of 5,000 people for the American Heart Association, I thought I did horrible. But I ended up being hired to emcee more events for the rest of the year. The more public speaking I did, the better I got at it. This is how I learned to value every step on the way to becoming great at something. My experience trying out for a Disney commercial, being rejected, and then being chosen for a role I didn't even know existed taught me that there are no dead ends in life as long as you keep trying. If you apply yourself, and you are willing to get down and dirty to really learn the ropes of whatever it is you want to do, you will find your way on the path that is meant for you.

"You don't have to be great to start, but you have to start to be great."

Zig Ziglar

Chapter 12

Hope is Alive

As I began to see results in terms of weight loss and my health improving when I decided to eat healthy and change my life, everything else started to click for me. I realized the importance of creating a plan of action for every area of my life. When I started my weight loss journey, I was unemployed, so the next thing I knew I needed to tackle was how I was going to support myself.

My entrepreneurial skills kicked into gear. I had hope that if I could change one part of my life, then I could change any part of my life. To do that, I created a production company (Papa Joe Networks) and a clothing line (JOE JOE) in order to embrace my passions for fashion, television and music production.

Creating these businesses was a part of developing the superhero inside, learning to shine bright and being who I felt I was meant to be. I had been in LA for seven years at the time I started the production company, and I knew my way around Hollywood. I knew the dynamics of getting a production company off the ground, and I knew who I needed to network with to make it happen.

As I changed my life and changed my eating habits, my career started to develop in different, more positive ways. Far more important than any of the money I've made with any of my businesses is the fact that I am truly happy and grateful that I get to do what I do every day.

When I was working in the corporate world, I hated my job. I hated getting up every morning. And let me tell you, if you start off every day in a negative state, you've got to do something to make a change.

If it's your job that breaks your spirit every morning, then you're in the wrong job. It's time to find something new. This is your LIFE we're talking about here. Your life is far more valuable than any amount of money.

In my former life, before I realized that I had control over the way I was living it, I was always focused on money. I really had no problem making it. I worked all the time, as much as I could. But even though I was making a lot of money, I wasn't enjoying it. It wasn't making me happy.

I had to find my way in my career. I had to find a way to bring balance into my career by doing something that I loved that also paid my bills. This is what everyone is looking for, and some people find it sooner than others. That's okay.

What's not okay is giving up the search and becoming focused on the wrong things to the point that you don't even

91

enjoy your life anymore. You have to keep hope alive that you will find what you love to do in your life and that it will support you.

I built up a lot of momentum in my life when I started exercising and eating better. I noticed a change in my energy levels. I noticed I had more confidence, and I just felt better. I didn't check my blood pressure or my weight every day because I could tell that what I was doing was working for me. I kept on believing that if I could take charge of my health, then I could take charge of any part of my life.

Whatever you're doing, whatever you're going after, whether it's a college degree, a job, a relationship, weight loss, or something else entirely, you've got to keep pursuing it and keep hope alive. You must keep hope in your heart.

Don't lose sight of it. Never stop listening, learning, loving and laughing. Never stop growing. Appreciate what you have and where you're at, even if you haven't made it to your end goal. Appreciating the struggle is just as important as appreciating being able to take hold of something you've been striving for.

In my life, having hope that I will reach my end goal keeps me moving. With every win I get, I become even more motivated to pursue something new and exciting I've never done before.

I'm always optimistic because I know there's always going to be another opportunity. There is no such thing as a dead end. If you have patience, you will be given another chance and shown another road for you to travel.

There are days when I want to quit pursuing my dreams. There are days when I want to go back on my lifestyle changes, and take a different ride. I've fallen off the wagon several times, but when that happens, I always remind myself that I've got to get back on. Life can be a balancing act like this sometimes. But when you keep putting yourself back on track when you slip up, eventually your balance gets better.

I don't want to get to 60 years old and have regrets. For me, that means acknowledging the importance of every aspect of my life. I don't want to be successful in one area of my life and failing in another. I've already gone down that road, and I found it very unfulfilling.

As humans, none of us are perfect. But we still have the ability to strive for what our own definition of "perfect" is. My goal is to live a life that I'm proud of and to be happy with who I am.

I want to always appreciate the little things more than the big things. I will always keep pushing forward, but not at the expense of my own peace of mind if things don't go my way. I'm not going to push emotionally and let it derail me. I'm always going to keep hope alive in my heart, and my wish is for you to do the same.

BALANCING THE SCALES

As you keep moving forward and pursuing your purpose, the fear and the butterflies will dissipate and fly away. I have already done more than I thought possible in my life. They say the sky is the limit, but I believe all of us can go past that and into the vast, limitless depths of space beyond.

All it takes is a little hope in your heart and the decision to never quit.

Message

As I began to see results from my weight loss efforts, I knew it was time to focus on improving my financial situation. This is when my entrepreneurial skills kicked in, and I started a production company and a clothing line. For a long time, I was miserable in my career even though I was making a lot of money. It took me awhile to find what I loved and what I was good at that would also pay my bills. But I believe that everyone can find this, and for some it just takes a little more time than others. If you keep hope alive in your heart, and you make the decision to never quit, I know that even the sky is not the limit for you. You are capable of so much more than you've ever imagined.

"Nothing will work unless you do."

Maya Angelou

Chapter 13

Out of Whack

When things get out of control in your life, you have to get back to the basics and remember what is important. You will face obstacles, even if you are living the life of your dreams. This is why I believe that true balance is learning how to deal with being out of balance.

In life, there is always something going on. There's always some kind of trouble. There's always something that needs to be addressed. As human beings, we're never in perfect sync. We have so many things to deal with in our daily lives.

Sometimes we focus in on one area of our lives so intensely that we forget about another. We can't do all things at once. But what we can do is learn to value our time and keep track of what we do with it.

Knowing what is at the top of your priority list is important. Not everything that you do in your life is of equal importance. You're the only one who can decide what's valuable to you and what isn't.

Some things you have to do can be automated or simplified if you find they're sucking up too much of your time. For example, when I was working extremely hard on my weight loss goals, I learned how to meal prep so I could save time during the week for other things and still stay on target with my health goals.

Because my meals were ready for me at every mealtime, this gave me more time to focus on business. The secret to finding balance is figuring out how to put your focus where it needs to be without losing touch with parts of your life that are important to you. Inevitably, you will lose your balance sometimes.

But when you discover something is out of balance, then you have to make an effort to change things. You might not make the perfect effort the first time, and that's okay. The important thing is that you're not ignoring that a change needs to happen in the first place.

To use the example of health again, if you start to notice that your pants are getting tighter, and your shirts are starting to fit a little too snug, then something is out of balance. The fit of your clothes is a sign that there's something you're doing that's affecting your health negatively, and you're going to have to make a change to put things in order.

If you're constantly having a bad day at work, and every day is a nightmare, there is no sense in just accepting that. If you hate your job, then there's likely an underlying reason. You might feel like you're being mistreated. You might not feel worthy of good pay or a good work environment. You may not feel respected. You may feel you're not doing good work.

The point is, with all these signs, you're seeing that you're not happy with what you're doing. You could be doing all the right things for all the wrong reasons, and that means that a shift needs to happen. You're going to continue to be out of balance until you do something about it.

For example, I'm taking steps to become whole in my own life in many areas. That includes my health and wellness, my career, my love life and my friendships. That doesn't mean I'm pushing myself over the limit in any one of these areas. I'm doing what I can do to slowly push the needle in the direction it needs to go.

When it comes to my love life, I'm not full-fledged going out to bars and trying to meet people every chance I can get. But what I can do while keeping my focus still on my health and my career is download a dating app, spend a few minutes each day seeing if I can find someone I'm interested in and want to get to know, and then move on.

My number one goal is just to take care of myself and do what I need to do to live a happy life. When it comes to the areas of my life where I'm not fully where I want to be, I keep hope alive. With hope in my heart, I know that I'm eventually going to succeed in these areas like I have in other areas of my life.

You don't have to have a perfect life in order for you to be perfectly happy. Balance is accepting your life for exactly what it is in this moment, but always doing your best to improve it every single day.

Message

Living a balanced life means learning how to accept that your life is always going to be out of balance in some way. As human beings, we have so many things on our plate, and we are never in perfect sync. But life always has a way of showing you when one area of your life is out of balance. The important thing to recognize is that you're going to continue to be out of balance until you do something about it. Once you recognize that there's an issue, it's your job to make change in that area of your life a priority. You don't have to have a perfect life to be perfectly happy, but you will be the happiest if you are doing your best to improve in some way every single day.

"Life is like riding a bicycle. To keep your balance, you must keep moving forward."

Albert Einstein

Chapter 14

Without Vision, You Are Nothing

I remember as a kid I uncovered some of what makes me happy in life to this day when I would go out on my bike and explore the neighborhood. This was my first taste of the adventure of life, with all of its surprises and joys. I will never give up pursuing what's next around the corner for me in my life. I choose every single day to look at life with a positive outlook, and that's what keeps me going.

That doesn't mean I haven't had my share of hardships. Even as a kid, I suffered every form of abuse, and it had a big effect on me. It contributed to the sense of self-loathing I dealt with as an adult.

Emotional abuse found its way into my relationships as an adult. One person I was with told me to my face that they made me fat on purpose so that no one else would want me. On another occasion, they told me that I was a terrible actor and I wasn't going to get the part as I headed out the door for an audition.

BALANCING THE SCALES

I was sexually abused by my friend's older brother when I was seven years old, and it took me a long time to even process what was going on. My parents' divorce was an ugly one and violence took place in my home. I suffered physical abuse at the hands of my biological father.

To keep moving towards my vision for my life, a life of adventure and joy, I had to learn to let all of this shit go. I had to come out of my funk, and come out of my shell. I had to break free.

I did this by staring at myself in the mirror and asking myself why I was unhappy. The next step was to learn how to put my life back into balance. That meant freeing myself from toxic habits, people and emotions that were dragging me down.

When I decided that it was time to finally put myself first in my life, I had to end a seven year relationship. After I broke things off, it was devastating for a little while because I was alone. But I soon realized that I was free because I didn't have to deal with the emotional abuse that was so prevalent in our relationship.

I was still unemployed, overweight and lonely. So even though I knew that breaking the relationship off was the right thing to do, it felt like my career, my health and my relationships were all crashing down around me. I had to figure out a way to prioritize my time to start putting things back together and building a happier life.

To do this, my motto became, "Take care of yourself first before you take care of anybody else." This is the same advice I give to anyone who asks me for help. You have to be willing to put yourself first because no one can do that for you. It's a personal decision, and you're the only one who can make it for yourself.

If putting yourself first means you have to wake up an hour earlier to take care of you, do it. Take time out of every single day just for yourself. You're the only you that you've got.

When you make time for yourself first thing every morning, you make sure this gets done. Whatever you've got to do, whether it's working out or developing yourself in some other way, when you get a jump on it in the morning, it changes the whole feel of the day. You feel so much better because you put yourself first.

Your vision for who you want to become in your life will guide to what you need to do during your "me time" every day. Once again, only you can create the vision. You won't find it out there. It's all in the heart.

One of my favorite games is chess. And in chess, every individual piece has its place. The same is true in life. Every individual person has their place. Sometimes you have to play the pawn, and sometimes you have to play the queen. But either way you have to protect your kingdom, and your kingdom is truly whatever you make of it through your vision for your life.

One of my favorite pieces of art that I own is a painting of a lighthouse that says on it, "Without vision, you are nothing." Your vision, just like a lighthouse for a ship at sea, is what will enable you to navigate through the storms of life to safety and happiness.

Throughout all of my life, the one thing I've learned for sure is that no matter the struggle or obstacle that's in front of you, there is a solution for it. I feel that I've gone through enough struggles in my life to be able to offer this advice to you with 100% confidence. You can truly get through anything. There is always a solution. Don't ever give up hope!

Message

As a kid, I uncovered some of what makes me happy in life when I used to go exploring on my bike in my neighborhood. But I lost touch with this desire for adventure when I suffered physical, sexual and mental abuse throughout my life. I had to get back in touch with myself by learning how to let go of all the emotional baggage I carried around with me for years. This is why my motto became, "Take care of yourself first before you take care of anyone else." Your vision for your life will guide you towards what you need to do to take care of yourself. Take time to do what you need to do for yourself every morning to start your day. If you're facing any kind of obstacle, know that there is a solution for it. All of my experience in life has enabled me to say this with 100% confidence.

"Your past does not determine who you are. Your past prepares you for who you are to become."

Unknown

Chapter 15

Don't Stop Believin'

The lowest point I ever reached in my life was the day I had to pawn some jewelry for drugs. I had received the jewelry from a family member. It's sad to me that I had to pawn something for money just to keep my habit alive. But the person I was living with at the time was also a drug addict, and I thought I had to keep drugs around in order for us to be happy or even friendly together.

In contrast, one of my favorite moments in my life was when I got the opportunity to be on national TV for the very first time on *The Doctors* TV show. When I was invited to be on the show, I had already done a lot of different acting jobs and been on camera as an actor, but I hadn't been on camera as myself.

Going on TV to tell my story made me realize that all that I have gone through in my life wasn't just for my own learning, but that it could also be valuable to others. I realized that with all the knowledge I'd gained, I was well equipped to try to help other people with my story to the best of my abilities.

I realized that losing all the weight I had lost had taught me so much more about life than just what I should be eating. Knowing what to eat is not even half the battle of weight loss. The real battle is in the mind and in understanding how you're wired so you can change your life in a positive way.

What I learned on my weight loss journey was the power of focus, the importance of self-love and the importance of knowing how to break things down into small, manageable steps. I also discovered that when I really applied myself to accomplishing my goals, my world opened up. I came out of depression, and I continued to find more things to do and activities to enjoy.

After I started walking, I had the idea to start lifting some weights. So I grabbed a pair of 30-pound dumbbells and started doing arm curls with them every morning before my walks. As my health improved and I lost more and more weight, I started bike riding. After that I started hiking, and that eventually evolved into parasailing.

As I opened up my life to different possibilities, it felt like the more I focused on the simple things like just caring for myself, the more opportunities the world presented me with. I found that when I focused on what I really wanted to achieve on the inside, the outside things were given to me in ways I couldn't even imagine. At this point in time, I'm now doing and experiencing things I never thought I would be able to do.

BALANCING THE SCALES

I have a huge amount of respect for people who have taken on big roles in their lives, because one thing I understand is that with more power comes more responsibility. When you try to accomplish something big in your life, you have to know that you're going to make mistakes. And if the goal you're trying to achieve is worthwhile, the cost of making a mistake is going to be high.

But mistakes are never the end of the road. The beauty of life is that we all make mistakes, and it's how we choose to overcome them that really makes the difference.

Having obstacles to overcome in your life, even if they are of your own creation, does not mean you are inferior or any less capable of living a great life than someone else who seems to have always had it all together. The truth is that no one has it all together in every area of their life. Some struggles are just more visible to other people than others. We all have struggles, and we all have the capability to overcome them.

One thing we don't ever give ourselves enough credit for is our resilience. There's a certain level of endurance that all human beings have, and I sincerely believe that's worth celebrating.

The beautiful thing about life is that we have the opportunity to stand up for ourselves and make our lives how we want them to be. In the same way, as a true people person at heart, I see it as my responsibility to stand up for other people. I want to be a cheerleader for the people.

I want to be remembered for always uplifting other people. My motivation to do what I do every day and to live my life comes from everywhere and everyone. I'm inspired by it all. I'm inspired by people who work hard at McDonald's. I'm inspired by CEOs who have built incredible companies that serve so many people. And I'm inspired by every single one of you who is reading this book.

I know that every person in the world is fighting some kind of battle, even if they never tell a soul about it. If that's you, and you're feeling all alone in this moment, remember that you're not.

We all have low moments and high moments, and that's why I've shared mine with you throughout this book. It doesn't matter how many wrong choices you've made in your life. What matters is that you, like one of my favorite Journey songs says, "Don't stop believin'!"

Keep fighting for balance and success in your life. And whenever you hear this song, remember that Papa Joe is out there somewhere in the world doing the same. You're never alone!

ALL MY LOVE, Papa Joe.

Message

We all experience highs and lows in our lives. We have all made good choices and bad choices. The important thing is how we overcome our mistakes. Every single person in the world is fighting some kind of battle, even if they never tell anyone about it. The beautiful thing about life is that we have the opportunity to stand up for ourselves and make our lives how we want them to be, regardless of the struggles we've had in the past. We are resilient creatures, and this needs to be celebrated! Keep fighting for balance and success in your life, and like the Journey song says, "Don't stop believin'!" I certainly believe in you, and I know you have it in you to do great things!

"Dear Past, thank you for all the lessons. Dear Present, let it be. Dear Future, I am ready!"

Unknown

THANK YOU

I want to say a big thank you to my friends and family. Actually, a thank you can't even begin to be enough to show my gratitude for everything that I've received from you all throughout my journey. It seems like at every turn, there was always someone cheering me on, sending me well wishes, words of encouragement, or lending me an ear when I needed to talk. I definitely could not have accomplished what I have alone. Each and every one of you has touched my life in such a way, and given me an overwhelming feeling of love. Thank you for being those people to me. I truly appreciate you, and I hope this book will inspire you, as you have inspired me.

MUCH LOVE!

In addition, this book is dedicated to the woman who brought me into this world, my mother. Thank you for being a source of love and the light that has shined on me since day one!

Love ya, Mom!

55409997R00065

Made in the USA
Columbia, SC
15 April 2019